Dolly West's Kitchen

Frank McGuinness was born in Buncrana, Co. Donegal, and now lives in Dublin and lectures in English at University College Dublin. His plays include: *The Factory Girls* (Abbey Theatre, Dublin, 1982), *Baglady* (Abbey, 1985), *Observe the Sons of Ulster Marching Towards the Somme* (Abbey, 1985; Hampstead Theatre, London, 1986), *Innocence* (Gate Theatre, Dublin, 1986), *Carthaginians* (Abbey, 1988; Hampstead, 1989), *Mary and Lizzie* (RSC, 1989), *The Bread Man* (Gate, 1991), *Someone Who'll Watch Over Me* (Hampstead, West End and Broadway, 1992), *The Bird Sanctuary* (Abbey, 1984) and *Mutabilitie* (RNT, 1997). His versions include Ibsen's *Rosmersholm* (RNT, 1987), *Peer Gynt* (Gate, 1988; RSC and international tour, 1994), *Hedda Gabler* (Roundabout Theatre, Broadway, 1994) and *A Doll's House* (Playhouse Theatre, Broadway, 1997); Chekhov's *Three Sisters* (Gate and Royal Court, 1990) and *Uncle Vanya* (Field Day Production, 1995); Lorca's *Yerma* (Abbey, 1987); Brecht's *The Threepenny Opera* (Gate, 1987) and *The Caucasian Chalk Circle* (RNT, 1997); Sophocles' *Electra* (Donmar and Broadway); and Ostrovsky's *The Storm* (Almeida).

FRANK McGUINNESS

Dolly West's Kitchen

faber and faber

First published in 1999
by Faber and Faber Limited
3 Queen Square, London WC1N 3AU

Typeset by Country Setting, Kingsdown, Kent CT14 8ES
Printed in England by Mackays of Chatham plc, Chatham, Kent

A CIP record for this book
is available from the British Library

ISBN 0-571-20370-1

2 4 6 8 10 9 7 5 3 1

Dolly West's Kitchen was premièred by the Abbey Theatre, Dublin, on 1 October 1999, with the following cast:

Dolly West Donna Dent
Rima West Pauline Flanagan
Esther Horgan Catherine Byrne
Justin West Michael Colgan
Ned Horgan Simon O'Gorman
Anna Owens Lucianne McEvoy
Alec Redding Anthony Calf
Marco Delavicario Perry Ojeda
Jamie O'Brien Harry Carnahan

Director Patrick Mason
Designer Joe Vanek
Lighting Nick Chelton
Fight Director Richard Ryan

For Phenie Franklin Mac Gabhann

Characters

Dolly West, in her thirties
Rima West, her mother, in her sixties
Esther Horgan, her older sister, in her late thirties
Justin West, her brother, in his twenties
Ned Horgan, Esther's husband, in his forties
Anna Owens, the Wests' maid, in her late teens
Alec Redding, in his late thirties
Marco Delavicario, in his twenties
Jamie O'Brien, Marco's cousin, in his twenties

Place

Buncrana, County Donegal, near the border with Derry

Time

During World War II

SETTING

The Wests live in a large, comfortable three-storey
house that overlooks the beach and is near the pier.

It is immaculately clean, well-presented and colourful.

To one side of the house there is a very large garden
that is being thoroughly utilised and well tended.

The herb garden is the only part of this visible on stage,
but it stretches to include substantial vegetable patches,
fruit-bearing trees and bushes and chicken coops.

At the centre of the stage is the kitchen itself.

The kitchen is dominated by a large, well-scrubbed
wooden table.

The living room, called the good room, is upstairs,
out of sight.

The family live in the kitchen. If at all possible,
the table should represent the heart of the kitchen.

There will be an obvious need for chairs, cutlery, glasses,
mugs, etc., but nothing should detract from the table.

To the other side of the kitchen is the shore and the sea.

The house is always present to the sound of the sea,
and between Act Two, Scene One and Scene Two
the whole stage is transformed into a shore/seascape.

It might be possible, if useful, to begin the play
with that shore/seascape lifting to reveal
the kitchen and its immediate environs.

Act One

SCENE ONE

There is a large white bowl on the table. Dolly West cracks an egg into the bowl. Anna stirs the egg. There are scones of bread on the table.

Dolly Beat the egg gently.

Anna Am I doing it too fast?

Dolly Yes. Take your time.

Anna It makes a lovely colour, the yolk and the white. Is this egg Hetty's?

Dolly How would I know?

Anna Your mother knows them all by name. Great name, Hetty the hen, isn't it? She's my favourite. She knows her own mind. If she wants to lay an egg, she will. Have I beaten it enough?

Dolly Stir it once more – for luck.

Anna How is that lucky?

Dolly An old Italian custom – they do it for wedding cakes. Do the same with all the other eggs, one by one.

Anna Did you love Italy, Miss West?

Dolly I wasn't in it long enough. Six or seven years in Florence, and I'm home four years now. I'm beginning to forget it. I loved Florence all right. Running a restaurant there was rough work. You begin to forget the reason for going to live there in the first place.

Anna Why did you go there?

Dolly I studied the history of European painting in university. I wanted to learn more. No better place than Italy.

During all of this Anna is breaking and stirring the eggs.
  Dolly has started to sort out herbs and different leaves of lettuce.
  She expertly eyes them, but disregards little, leaving them to soak in a white basin of water. What she keeps she washes thoroughly, laying them to dry on a yellow dishcloth.

Anna I'd love to go to Italy and get married by the Pope. Beautiful. The only thing would ruin it is wearing black on your wedding day.

Dolly Black?

Anna A black mantilla. All women have to wear it meeting the Pope. Imagine destroying a white wedding dress with that contraption on your head instead of a veil.

Dolly Will you wear a veil, Anna?

Anna With the rationing these days? Miss West, I know a girl saving to get married next Boxing Day, she asked her mother about getting a veil. Her ma said she would be lucky to pull the skin of her arse over her head.

Dolly Will you marry, Anna?

Anna With all those American soldiers stationed across the border in Derry? They're the last word. They come over to the Republic when they're on leave and they're not supposed to, but the women all latch on to them. Even if they weren't gallivanting about and I didn't get married, it wouldn't be for want of asking.

Dolly I'm sure it wouldn't. You're a lovely girl, Anna.

Anna beams with pleasure.

Anna I'm not – I'm wild-looking.

Dolly You're a beautiful girl, Anna. (*She carefully seasons the eggs.*)

Anna Why did you never marry, Miss West?

Dolly I was never one for walking down the aisle.

Anna But you've stepped out with fellas – in your day? Between the two of us?

Dolly I might have – in my day – and I might have done more than stepping out. Between the two of us.

Anna Miss West, if a fella you take a shine to asks you for a feel, should you let him?

Dolly Feel what?

Anna You know yourself.

Dolly No, I don't know.

Anna You must know.

Dolly I don't.

Anna Jesus, you must at your age.

Dolly Is it your nose? Feel your nose, pick your nose?

Anna What?

Esther enters by the shore.

Dolly Anna, if any man wants to pick your nose, don't let him. It's a disgusting habit.

Anna I wouldn't let anybody pick my nose.

Dolly Then you're a wise woman.

Esther comes into the kitchen.

Anna I think you've spent too long in Italy, Miss West. Men don't do that here.

Dolly A credit to Irish manhood.

Esther What's to Irishmen's credit?

Dolly They don't pick women's noses.

Esther They would if there was a bottle of Guinness up them.

Anna I happen to think Irishmen are a credit to their country.

Esther You should marry one. I happen to think they're full of it.

Anna Full of what?

Esther Raspberry jam. Imagine your wedding night, Anna. You're lying there looking at the ceiling and he comes at you with his cockadoodledandy. (*She makes the sound of an explosion.*) He covers you in raspberry jam. It's the happiest day of your life.

Dolly I'll tell that Ned Horgan on you.

Esther You tell my husband what you like.

Anna I think Mr Horgan is a good man.

Esther An excellent man. An excellent soldier. Defending Ireland from invasion, a neutral man in a neutral army protecting his neutral wife.

Dolly Anna, my mother's in the garden – see if she wants tea.

Anna exits.

Watch that mouth of yours – Anna's no more than a child.

4

Esther I can't help what I say. My mind's on this war. We're living in a port, Dolly. Buncrana is a port. Our beloved leader, De Valera, has warned this part of the country they might invade us for our ports, coming at us from all sides, the English, the Germans and the Yanks. The English we've dealt with before – we can deal with them again. What about the Germans?

Dolly Start praying it's the English.

Esther And the Yanks?

Dolly They're full of raspberry jam – full of it – we could eat them all.

Esther Now I could eat a horse. What are you cooking?

Dolly Eggs just – and a salad.

Esther Lovely. Justin and Ned are eating with us.

Dolly I thought they'd be eating in Dunree fort. I've no meat for them. They'll be like bears.

Esther Let them eat what's put in front of them. There's plenty of scone bread to feed them.

Dolly The men will want potatoes at least.

Esther Jesus, you'd think they were royalty.

Dolly Anna, dig us some spuds from the garden.

Anna calls offstage.

Anna All right.

Dolly Did you find Mammy?

Rima enters the herb garden.

Rima What did you mean, did you find Mammy? Was I lost or what? Where was she to look for me – under a gooseberry bush?

5

Esther Need a right size of gooseberry bush to find you under it.

Rima Maybe it was the one you crawled out from?

Esther Did you really find me there, Mammy?

Rima You're a bit long in the tooth to believe that, aren't you? You know well how I got you. A coal boat came to the pier and it delivered you. I washed you. I dried you, I clothed you in silk, Esther, my eldest born. Look at you now – I should have dumped you back in the water. Dolly, are we eating eggs again? I want none of that green stuff floating about in that bowl.

Dolly Mother, that's herbs.

Rima Mother, that's shite. The amount of grass and leaves we eat in this house – it's not natural. That whore Hitler's doing me out of a bit of stewing beef. The men won't eat that. I won't either.

Dolly You have to eat – if it's not eggs, what do you want?

Rima A slice of the cat's arse, please.

Dolly You've cut that many slices off the cat, it has no arse left.

Rima Maybe in fancy Italy you ate cats. This is Ireland. We've known true hunger. A hundred years ago we *were* eating the very grass. Now Dolly West is doing it to us again. Look at the face on her. She's so miserable you'd swear she was a Derry woman.

Dolly Thank you very much.

Rima Say what you like about this war, the siege of Derry was worse. They were eating the rats. Lundy sold the city for the sake of a bun. That's how starving they were, the Derry people. Of course, at that time they were all Protestant. I've always heard it prophesied we'll see them begging again with their mouths open for bread.

Dolly Who prophesied that?

Rima Our Lady when she appeared in Moville. Years before yous were born. They got very big-headed about that. Then Our Lord Jesus Christ appeared around the shore front in Buncrana. That put a stop to Molville's gallop.

Esther What did he prophesy?

Rima How would I know? He didn't appear to me. The one who did see him, she wasn't much use – she was deaf and dumb.

Esther Could she talk and hear afterwards?

Rima They say she could but who knows? She was put into a convent, or maybe it was a mental home? I don't know. I will have a mouthful of those eggs, even if they kill me.

Dolly I might find you a rat to go with them.

Rima The eggs will be enough to poison me.

Dolly Mother dear, I would not poison you. That would be too slow.

Rima What did you say?

Esther She said you were getting a bit slow – a bit old.

Rima She'll still feel the whack of my fist if she doesn't watch herself.

Justin and Ned enter from the garden, Ned in sergeant's uniform, Justin in officer's.

Ned Who are you threatening, Rima?

Rima You and all the Irish army put together, Sergeant Horgan. Good afternoon, Justin, darling son, head buckcat of the Irish army.

Rima sings the opening lines of the Irish National Anthem.
   Justin grunts, opens his newspaper, sits and reads it. Ned cuts a slice of scone bread, butters it and eats.

Good afternoon, how are you, Mother? I'm well, son, is there anything in the paper? A plague of killer bees are heading towards Buncrana. Son, what will the Irish army do? Give us all your sheets, Ma, we'll spread syrup over them and hang them on the washing lines! That way you'll be saved. And so will we, the men of Ireland, because of my mammy's syrup. My son, Justin, my son the officer – he has brains to burn. Honest to Jesus, other women give birth to children. I gave birth to three mad whores, one uglier than the other.

Justin I am not ugly.

Esther We are not ugly.

Rima Thank Christ I'll never have to marry any of yous. Dolly, ask your brother, the colonel-in-chief, why he has a face like a hatchet?

Anna enters with a basin of washed potatoes. Dolly starts to examine them.

Dolly What's wrong with you, Justin?

Justin Nothing wrong as yet. Have you not got the spuds on? We haven't got all day for our dinner.

Dolly Less than twenty minutes they'll boil. Why are you like a bear with a sore head?

Ned We had a phone call at the fort this morning. It was from your old pal Alec Redding, Dolly.

Dolly Alec – where is he?

Ned Across the border – stationed in Derry. He's in the British army.

Dolly I guessed that much. Why's he in Derry?

Ned Working with the Americans – some kind of interpreter.

Dolly The Americans speak English.

Justin That's a matter of opinion.

Rima I cannot follow what the Yanks are saying in films. I spent the whole of *Gone with the Wind* getting Esther to tell me what are they saying – what are they saying?

Esther Will I ever forget it?

Rima What was wrong with Vivien Leigh anyway, wanting that drink of water, Leslie Howard – what was wrong with her? She had Clark Gable . . .

Justin We were talking about Alec Redding.

Rima When is he coming down to see us?

Ned Well, he would definitely like to –

Dolly Of course, he will. Alec was always welcome –

Justin Was.

Dolly What do you mean 'was'?

Justin No man will be welcome here wearing the uniform of the British army. If you all want to meet, take the train to Derry. Meet him across the border in the so-called Northern Ireland.

Dolly So you're now decreeing who sits in this kitchen?

Justin No British soldier will come under this roof. It's bad enough we have to tolerate them in the North.

They've laid claim to that, but not for much longer after the war's over.

Dolly Justin, this is Alec.

Justin I don't care if it's God almighty.

Anna I wouldn't worry about him being in uniform, Mr West. If the soldiers cross into the Republic, they have to wear civvies. The British soldiers are very good about it. The Yanks, though, you always see them in uniform. I don't blame them. Their trousers are gorgeous.

Justin When I ask for your opinion, you can open your mouth. Gorgeous trousers.

Dolly Did Alec say when he'd come down?

Ned The weekend – Saturday or Sunday.

Justin Are you going to defy me?

Dolly Defy you? Who do you think you are, pup?

Justin The man of this house who chooses not to let an enemy soldier into his house.

Esther His house –

Justin An Irishman who does not want the English anywhere.

Dolly I didn't know you'd signed your house away, Mother.

Rima I haven't.

Dolly Then what do you say?

Rima I couldn't give a tinker's curse who comes in here, just as long as they don't attack me in my bed. Mind you, Alec's not a bad looking man. He can attack me wherever he likes.

Justin You're setting some example, Ma. Many Irishwomen were attacked in their beds by British soldiers.

Rima And many were throwing their leg over more than a bicycle.

Justin You should be ashamed –

Rima Son dear, would you get off your knees praying and dance? It would be the life of you. Why are you not out chasing women?

Silence.

Justin Dolly, if you welcome Alec into this house –

Dolly If you don't welcome him, you don't eat. Starting now, you starve, boy.

Justin Throw your dinner into the fire. The fire –

Ned Justin, be a good man, sit down and eat –

Justin Are you telling me what to do?

Silence.

I asked you, sergeant. Are you telling me what to do?

Ned I'm not, no.

Justin No, what?

Ned No, sir.

Justin We have important surveys to do this afternoon. I'll see you at the fort. (*He gathers his newspaper.*)

Dolly You'll be calling into the chapel, I'm sure, Justin. Maybe you should pray you'll stop turning into such a cruel little shit.

Justin Maybe you should just call into the chapel, Dolly. The one time only in the four years you're back home. I'd say you're the first Irish Catholic who lived in Italy and came back a heathen. Enjoy your dinner. I hope it chokes you, you selfish old bitch. You never listen to me. You never have.

He exits.
Esther wanders onto the shore and lights a cigarette.
Dolly goes out to join her.
Ned cuts more bread and eats.

Rima Do you know what we'll do this afternoon, Anna? Dig up that gooseberry bush in Dolly's garden. I wish I'd done it forty years ago. Young ones put years on you, Ned. You're lucky not to have them.

Ned We still might.

Dolly What way is the army hardening Justin? What is he becoming? He was the gentlest boy. We were worried he was too soft. But I don't like this. He shouldn't have said that.

Esther And Ned should have stood up to him. But he won't. He never will.

Rima So Alec's back.

Dolly What would Ned like to eat this evening?

Esther Forget about Ned. That's not what you're thinking about.

Rima I wonder this time will he make a move.

Dolly Alec's my business, Esther, mind your own.

Esther Do you know what I'd like? Sail the Atlantic – swim across it. But I won't. You made the break and left, Dolly. I never did.

Dolly Much good it did me. Come in and eat, Esther.

Esther In a minute. I have my business to attend to.

Dolly goes back to the kitchen.
Esther stands smoking, listening to the sea.

Jesus – Jesus – Jesus.

The sound of the sea increases.

SCENE TWO

Dolly is ironing on the table.
Anna is sorting out dried laundry.
Ned is polishing a pair of boots that are already shining.

Anna You should be getting Mrs Horgan to clean your boots for you, sergeant.

Ned Some chance of that, eh Dolly?

Dolly smiles.

Anna If you were my man, I'd do it for you.

Ned You'll make someone a great wife, Anna.

Anna Everybody says that.

They continue working in a brief silence.

Will I run up the street and see if Mrs West and Mrs Horgan need a hand to carry down the messages?

Dolly You'll stroll up no street. Go and freshen up that room in case Mr Redding wants to stay the night.

Anna Right, Miss West. (*She leaves.*)

Ned How long since you saw Alec?

Dolly Four – five years ago – before the war. I've had the occasional letter from him. He stayed with me in Florence for about a month before he went on his wanderings. He was heading for Tibet.

Ned What the Christ would take him there?

Dolly Alec all over.

Ned Going out foreign – I don't know how yous do it. Even going into Derry, I feel like a stranger.

Dolly Don't let Justin hear that or he'll drum you out of the army. God, it's hard to imagine Alec in uniform, following orders. He was always his own man.

Ned Alec's not the kind of man to shirk his duty to his country.

Dolly He's spent more time out of England than in it. When we were at Trinity, he never took a holiday back there. Even Christmas he spent wandering through blizzards in the west of Ireland.

Ned You never came home when you were in Italy.

Dolly Too far to travel.

Ned Esther did it – to see you. All on her own. I couldn't face the journey. Do you miss it?

Dolly Funny what you miss. Smell of the bread. The taste of the water. The sky some nights, with a single star in it. The restaurant was going grand. Hard work, but I was learning all the time. Packed most nights. Every night. But I was always the Irishwoman, Ned. That was their nickname for me. The stranger. Even at the height of summer, the nights were cold. I used to take a hot water bottle to bed with me always. Fill it in the kitchen, throw it over my shoulder, walk up the stairs. One night it burst scalding water down my back – I could barely walk. That was the night I turned the key to my door and came home.

Ned Why?

Dolly Bad luck. Evil. Mussolini and his boys. A sign. Scalding water. Run like hell, before hell catches you. You wouldn't want to know Italy, Ned, before the war.

Ned What are the Italians like?

Dolly The best. But they have a sad streak in them, and it's savage.

Ned Like ourselves.

Dolly No – they're not.

Ned Esther loved it.

Dolly She did when she came home. She didn't when she was there. The ever changeable Esther. For all the long years I've known my sister I still declare the woman to be a mystery. She's the one supposed to be like our father. If he'd lived longer, we might have known him better, and her. A mystery.

Ned She's hardly sleeping at all now. She's always walking on the shore.

Dolly She never slept much and she loves the water. You know that.

Ned She's talking to herself as well. I hope she's not getting a want in the head.

Dolly Nothing's wrong with the same one's head.

Ned She has nothing to do. You and Anna do all about the house.

Dolly Her job is to manage the money. That lady can make a pound go a very long way. She has every shopkeeper terrified.

Ned That part-time teaching job – she should never have stopped it.

Dolly She hated the school – truth to tell, she hated the children.

Ned No, she didn't. She did not.

Silence.

She did not hate the children.

Silence.
Alec has entered the herb garden, carrying a large bag.
He surveys the whole garden.

Dolly Ned, I've never said this, and I might regret it, but did you ever think of moving her out of this house?

Ned Into the married quarters at Dunree fort? You can't swing a cat in them. This is a grand big house. More than enough room. Your da, Dr West, left a fair whack of money. Esther's used to that way of living. What could I offer her?

Dolly Esther will be like our mother – getting worse with age, but that might make her better.

Ned You said she was like your father, and he did a runner, didn't he?

Silence

Dolly He came back, didn't he?

Ned To die.

Dolly As good enough reason as any.

Alec speaks in an Irish accent.

Alec Excuse me, lady of the house, but would you have a cup of tea for a stranger?

Dolly The worst Irish accent in the world – Alec!

He comes to embrace her.
She has just been folding a shirt.
She presses it against him as they embrace.
She smells his shoulder.
He kisses her forehead.
She whispers.

Dolly I've missed you.

Alec Mutual.

He turns to Ned, who has his boot in his hand.
He goes to shake Ned's hand.
Ned drops the boot.
They shake hands and nearly embrace.

Alec Mr Horgan.

Ned Mr Redding. Rest your feet – sit down. Didn't you hear the man, Dolly West? He wants a cup of tea.

Dolly He'll get it.

Alec I think I can do better than tea, Mr Horgan – (*He produces a bottle of rum from the bag.*)

Ned Mr Redding, my favourite old grog. The bottle of rum. You remembered. Alec, you're as decent an eejit as ever looked over a half-door. Now I'm going to break your heart, bucko. I have to go to work. So I can't have one with you.

Alec But we will tonight, lad. We will tonight.

Ned I'd say we might, if we're let. Dolly West runs a very tight ship – who knows – after lights out and she's tucked up tight, who knows what badness might be afoot?

Dolly If you two boyos think you're in for a feed of drink without me in the middle of you, think again. Ned, off you go, and God save Ireland, said the heroes.

Ned God save Ireland, said the men.

Dolly You'll be poisoned talking to Alec before the evening's out.

Ned has pulled on his boots.
  He looks at his hands and then touches Alec's hands.

Ned Jesus, polish all over my hands. Did I get it on yours as well?

Alec Don't worry about it.

Ned I'll run them under the outside pump. Good luck, Alec.

Alec I'll see you, Ned.

They gently punch each other in the stomach.
  Ned exits.

Dolly I don't know what you do to Ned Horgan, but you always fill him with life. It's good to see you, Alec, you old rogue.

Alec Rogue – is that the best you can rise to?

Dolly You get no more. Those days are long gone. You think I was going to spend my days trailing after your favours to Tibet?

Alec Tibet – was that where I was going the last time? It was – yes. You were right not to trail me. I did have a romantic interlude there, in a manner of speaking.

Dolly You were going to marry a Tibetan? What would mummy have said?

Alec Immediately onto marriage and mothers – Miss Dolly West. Anyway, we pitched camp in a quite remote area, and the natives were charming, very generous and welcoming. We were about to hit the sack, when this little girl – six or seven – she arrived with her yak. It was all decorated with bells and ribbons. We patted it and told her it was a lovely yak. She made it clear the yak expected more than patting.

Dolly She thought you were going to –

Alec Yes, with a yak.

Dolly You've had your fair share of dogs –

Alec That's enough. We got rid of her and the yak, or so we thought. She was back five minutes later with a younger yak that had no need of bells or ribbons. We sent that one packing as well, but I'm sure that somewhere in Tibet there's an ageing yak sipping gin with smeared lipstick thinking those bloody English turned me down for a younger model.

Dolly Jesus, I'm ageing with the yak.

Alec Dolly, you don't look a day over thirty – in yak years.

Dolly Watch it. You came home to join the army?

Alec I did. Quite a journey – some dicey moments – tell you about them later. I got home and signed up. My father wanted to land me a job in intelligence –

Dolly You never finished your degree in medicine, Alec –

Alec Don't be rude. I never wanted to, Dolly. I didn't want it, I was looking for danger – you know me – and I got it.

Dolly Danger? You're stationed in Derry, Alec.

Alec True, but I'm also nanny to a gang of extremely lively American boys, and while I can hit on many of our acquaintances who would think they had died and gone to heaven if they were in my position, the fresh smell of cock has not been to my liking since I was fifteen.

Dolly You had a fling with a man in your twenties.

Alec I was drunk.

Dolly It went on for three months.

Alec I was very drunk. I have not been similarly tempted. So I'm here to explain your ways to them. They have caused havoc wherever they have been posted.

Dolly Welcomed with open legs.

Alec And every other orifice. The powers that be saw I studied at Trinity College, presumed me to be a Dubliner, posted me here and I have to save them from the natives. Forgive me for using that word.

Dolly We are natives, Alec.

Alec Don't say that, Dolly – it doesn't sound terribly nice coming from you. Where is everybody? Where's your mad mother and your even madder sister? Where's the beautiful broth of a boy, Justin?

Dolly He's in the Irish army.

Alec Justin? Ten years ago he'd destined himself to the church. I thought he would be Pope by now.

Dolly He settled to be an officer in the Irish army. It came as no surprise. The child thrives on rules and regulations.

Alec Like yourself, Dolly. Number one rule – if you do something, do it perfectly. Number one regulation, don't do it for too long. Don't come back – unless it's to the old sod of Ireland.

Dolly For the duration of the war. I didn't fancy facing either side in Italy – yours or theirs.

Alec What happened to your restaurant?

Dolly Boarded up – hope it's still standing.

Alec The woman who couldn't boil an egg as a student –

Dolly We always had maids, we still do –

Alec And you call me a snob. Something for you. I raided Uncle Sam's pantry.

Dolly Alec, we're grand down here in the Republic. The rationing is not as severe as it is in the North. We have meat and butter –

Alec Not this. (*From his bag he produces two bottles of wine.*)

Dolly You'll be shot.

He produces two more.

I'll turn Protestant for you.

He produces two more.

I'm fetching you our yak, darling. (*She calls out.*) Anna, I want you – where are you?

Anna calls offstage.

Anna Hanging out clothes on the line. I'm finished – I'm coming. (*She rushes in with a large basket.*)

Dolly This is Mr Redding. This is Anna, who works for us. Anna Owens.

Alec You're much prettier than a yak, child.

Anna A what?

Alec Forgive my rudeness. How do you do?

They shake hands.

Anna My hands are all wet from the washing.

Dolly Put than wine in the basket.

Anna does so.

Break one and I'll break you. Run up the town and see your pals after that. Don't stuff yourself with fish and chips. You're eating good food here. Be back soon.

Anna I will, Miss West. Goodbye, sir. You didn't wear your uniform.

Alec No, I'm afraid I didn't.

Anna You look good in what you're wearing. Your shoes are lovely.

Alec You notice clothes – men's clothes?

Anna I notice the men wearing them. Does he think Irishwomen are stupid?

Alec I'm sorry I spoke.

Anna I didn't mean to be bad mannered. Sorry.

Dolly Run on, Anna.

Anna exits, carrying the basket carefully.

Alec God, she sounds exactly like you when you first came to Dublin.

Dolly My accent hasn't changed that much.

Alec As much as you have, Dolly. She has the same cheek, that girl. You must breathe it in the air here.

Dolly Just as well – would you change us?

Esther rushes into the garden, shouting Dolly's name.

Jesus, what's wrong? Esther, has my mother had one of her turns? Is she all right?

Esther enters the kitchen.

Esther Your mother has not had a turn. Your mother has made a show of herself. She has shamed me for the last time. She is no longer any mother of mine. I disown her. (*She sees Alec.*) Alec, we were expecting you. Tell me, have I changed?

Alec No, Esther, you remain yourself.

Esther I'm only sorry you're here to see me murdering my mother, but at least you can say you saw me before I was hanged.

Alec What did she do to deserve being stretched by the neck until she's dead?

Esther I was arguing in the Co about the tea ration, she slipped away from me. I heard her muttering something about saying a prayer in the grotto. Our mother's grotto is nobody else's, Alec.

Alec It's the Crushkeen pub in the middle of the town. The snug. I remember.

Esther She's a glass to her lips, drinking when I walk in there, with two young American soldiers. My mother is getting drunk with two G.I.s. I'm not – she is. She has also invited them back here to eat with us. What's Justin going to say? You heard the outburst about Alec –

Alec Outburst?

Dolly Never mind.

Esther He doesn't want you in here because you're a British soldier now, Alec. I'm sorry –

Alec The shit.

Dolly Esther, your mouth –

Esther Should be cemented shut.

Anna Do you want me to leave?

Dolly You do, I'll leave with you.

Rima, Marco and Jamie enter the herb garden. Marco and Jamie carry voluminous shopping bags.

23

Alec If I am causing any offence whatsoever, I assure you –

Dolly Alec, stop acting the Englishman.

Rima Hello – guess who's here?

Esther They've guessed.

Rima enters the kitchen.

Rima Did you tell them about the boys?

Esther Don't you talk to me.

Rima They're strangers in a foreign land. They could be your own brother if he was fighting in the war. We're feeding them.

Esther They were feeding you with plenty of drink.

Rima I didn't have to put my hand into my pocket. Americans know how to treat their women. They are wee angels. Well, big angels, Dolly, you'll love them. They are gods. Gods of men. Young fellas, come in – come in.

Marco and Jamie enter, still carrying the shopping bags.

Dolly Hello, lads.

Marco Hi – hi.

Jamie nods.

Rima Leave down them bags and take your rest. You're as welcome as the flowers of May to dear old Donegal.

Marco Your sister must have told you who we were.

Esther I said nothing – how did you know she was my sister?

Marco Did you also tell her I hated you on sight?

Esther May I ask why?

Marco The way you dress.

Esther What's wrong with it?

Marco Nothing, if you're posing for the Statue of Liberty.

Esther I've never seen the Statue of Liberty.

Marco It shows, honey.

Esther I'm not your honey.

Marco My God, that woman's hair – was it suicide?

Esther My hair is my crowning glory.

Marco Did she say crowning or clowning? I have such trouble with consonants.

Esther I'm going to wring his neck.

Marco I am Marco Delavicario. This is my Irish-American cousin, Jamie O'Brien. We signed up together. Jamie brought the clothes he was standing in and a change of underwear. I brought one taffeta dress and a change of high heels. Who knows what might happen in the heat of the battle?

Esther They let a man like you into the US army?

Marco Right now they'd let a man like you into the US army.

Esther At least I'm a real woman.

Marco May God forgive reality.

Jamie Do the proper introductions.

Marco You must be Miss Dolly West.

He kisses Dolly's hand, as does Jamie.
Marco puts his arm around Jamie.

Marco Your mother has told us so much about you. Tell me it's lies.

Dolly Completely.

Marco looks into Jamie's eyes.

Marco I adore that woman already. I worship her mother. I hate her sister. She's all yours. Captain Redding, we know – from our briefing session about the natives.

Dolly You do call us natives?

Alec I may have cracked a joke –

Marco We all know each other – isn't this divine?

Rima Marco has great stories about the film stars. Do your Jean Harlow mouth, Marco.

He does so.

Did you hear the one about Jean Harlow and the cucumber? You get a dish of honey –

Dolly Mother, not in mixed company. Wait until the men have gone.

Rima Alec, it's yourself.

Alec It is, Mrs West.

Rima Rima to you, Alec.

Alec Good to see you, Rima.

Rima You're alive, Alec. May you stay so. Hard fight ahead, God protect you. Dolly, I've asked these boys to eat with us.

Dolly The more the merrier – we have enough.

Anna enters the kitchen.

You didn't stay long in the town, Anna.

Anna There was nobody there. I saw yous ahead of me. (*She looks to Jamie.*) You must be worn out carrying the shopping bags. (*She looks to Jamie.*) Will I make you all tea?

Marco That would be delightful.

Alec A cup of tea would be lovely.

Esther Do you know tea is rationed?

Marco You can count Jamie out from drinking tea. He's a coffee man.

Rima He'll wait a long time before he sees coffee in this country.

Dolly Does your cousin ever speak?

Marco I'll ask, shall I? Jamie, do you ever speak?

Jamie I would like a glass of water.

Anna I can fetch you some spring well water. Lovely and cold.

Esther Like himself.

Jamie smiles at her.

Jamie And like you.

Esther I think he speaks.

Justin enters from the shore. He eyes Alec coldly and nods. Alec returns the greeting.

Justin Alec.

Alec Justin.

Justin Am I to be introduced to the other gentlemen?

Dolly This is my brother. Mr Delavicario – Mr O'Brien – Justin West.

Justin A right gathering of the Allies.

Marco Boys together – that's right.

Justin You've crossed the border.

Marco Hasn't everyone?

Justin I beg your pardon.

Marco Just being chatty.

Justin I never am.

Marco You can use your tongue for other matters.

Justin Than what?

Marco Chatting.

Justin Yankee wit.

Marco Yankee wisdom.

> *From this exchange to the end of the scene, Justin*
> *does not take his eyes off Marco.*
> > *Anna gives Jamie a drink of water.*
> > *He downs it in one go.*

Anna Isn't it lovely water?

Jamie Lovely. And cold.

Justin What are you doing in here – has the invasion begun?

Rima I invited them to eat with us. And they will – in my house, in my kitchen.

Justin Your kitchen? Are you sure, Ma? The word in the town is that this is Dolly West's kitchen. All soldiers welcome.

Dolly Whose word is that?

Justin Everybody's.

Dolly Then it must be right. So, welcome to you all. You'll eat tonight in Dolly West's kitchen.

Jamie Your beach looks very beautiful.

Esther It is beautiful.

Jamie Might we take a walk there?

Esther We might.

Justin I'll accompany my sister.

Marco I'll accompany my cousin.

Justin How courteous of you.

Marco Thank you, kind sir.

Anna Can I go for a walk, Miss West?

Dolly I need you to give me a hand.

Alec Let her, Dolly. Come along, Anna. I'll chaperone you. All these strong young fellows – I'll make sure you don't fall into temptation.

Anna Can I, Miss West?

Dolly Run on.

> *Anna takes Alec's arm.*
> *They exit to the beach.*
> *Jamie and Esther do likewise.*

Marco I shall refuse your arm, young man. I do not trust men in uniform.

Justin What the hell are you?

Marco An angel fallen from the skies.

Justin Where exactly are you from?

Marco Paradise.

Marco exits.

Justin Is he not right in the head? Is there anybody in this house right in the head?

Rima I don't think so, son.

Justin exits.
   Dolly and Rima look at each other.

I'm a bit tired. I'll have a wee rest before eating.

Dolly What are you doing, Ma?

Rima Me – doing what?

Dolly What have you brought into this house?

Rima Badness. Good, isn't it? A bit of badness.

SCENE THREE

It is evening, towards the end of supper, and wine is being drunk.
   Dolly dishes out wild strawberries from a white bowl.
   Anna serves them to the family and guests sitting around the table.
   On the table there is a skeleton of a large salmon and the bare remains of a chicken.
   There are also empty white vegetable dishes.
   The bowls Anna serves are also white.
   Marco helps Dolly and Anna serve and clear.
   Alec opens wine. Ned opens bottles of Guinness.

Dolly Lemons – that's what I really miss, Alec. Gorgeous lemons. God, I love the smell of them. That's what these strawberries lack. Just a little taste of lemon juice. So forgive the dessert.

Alec It will be great, Dolly.

Ned I'd say this war could last for another ten years. It could, sir – it could.

Rima Don't say that, Ned – you'll wish it on us.

Ned I wish no such thing on this unfortunate earth.

Dolly Was the salmon all right?

Alec Perfect.

Rima Before the war I wouldn't have thanked you for fish. Now we have to eat it.

Marco approaches Ned.

Marco I don't believe we have been formally introduced.

Ned I don't believe so, no.

Marco My name's Mary – Mary O'Shaughnessy.

Ned That's very unusual.

Marco Yes, isn't it? But all the men in my family are called O'Shaughnessy. (*He walks off.*)

Justin And you think your people might have migrated from here to the States, O'Brien?

Jamie My father said his father came from Donegal, but I don't know where.

Rima I think you overcooked the chicken, Dolly.

Anna I did the chicken, Mrs West.

Rima Then it was grand, pet.

Dolly It was grand if she cooked it, but not if I did?

Rima I'm only encouraging the child. You can say nothing to that one.

Justin If you're a Donegal man, you're true Irish. Ancient Irish. Just off the coast about ten mile north of here there's a patch of rock they say was the earliest formation of the island of Ireland.

Rima Who says that?

Justin Geologists, Ma.

Rima Enlighten me what they do.

Justin They study the rocks and soils of a place and they discover what formations shaped a country like Ireland into being.

Rima Jesus, I could tell you that myself. Everybody knows that. A little bit of heaven fell from out the skies one day, and when the angels found it, it looked so lovely there they sprinkled it with gold dust and they called it Ireland.

Justin For God's sake, Mother.

Rima Don't for God's sake me. I'm not the one saying it. It's the song says it – I'm only repeating –

Esther And you believe everything you hear in a song?

Rima Well, I believe that from where I'm sitting it's a long way to Tipperary, it's a long, long way to go.

Esther Where did we dig her out of?

Rima Listen to that. Never finished her education. It's an old saying and a true one. Shite flies high when it's hit with a stick. Where's the pepper for these strawberries?

Marco Well, Jamie, are the Irish as you hope to find them?

Jamie No.

Rima Enlighten us why?

Jamie I thought you might dance and sing, and have the neighbours in to play music.

The Irish look at each other and then at Jamie.

Rima Son, if any neighbour crossed my door with his banjo, the next time he plays it it will be with his arse. Alec, you're being very quiet this evening. Mind you, he always was. I always liked Alec. There's one nice thing I'll say about the English, when they keep their mouths shut, they're grand.

Dolly And they wonder why the League of Nations never worked.

Rima I'm saying nothing against anybody. Alec's more than welcome. All nations welcome in this kitchen. Didn't I ask these two American boys to eat with us? And I'm glad I did, even if one seems to be deaf and dumb, and the other one is definitely wearing lipstick.

Marco Madam, I am an American soldier. I am most emphatically not wearing lipstick. A little rouge, yes. No Nazi's going to bitch about my bone structure.

Justin Do you know what the Nazis do to men like you?

Marco Why the fuck do you think I'm fighting them?

Silence.

Ned Is that why you're called Mary?

Esther Who's called Mary?

Marco Everybody, sister.

Rima What's it like with two men in the bed?

Silence. They all look at her.

I'm only asking. There was a man like that here. Nice chap. A baker. That was years ago. The word was he had the biggest micky ever seen on any man in this town. Thirteen inches. It gave a whole new meaning to the baker's dozen.

Silence.

Can I say nothing this night?

33

Marco Would someone pour me a very large whiskey very gently?

Justin does so.

Rima I was only saying –

Dolly We heard.

Rima I remember he was a Methodist. I suppose I'm not allowed to say that as well. Mind you, apart from him, I never had much time for the Methodists.

Justin Why not, Ma?

Rima What did they ever do to free Ireland? I have nothing against Protestants as such. Then, I'm blessed. I can recognise one immediately and watch my mouth.

Alec How would you recognise I was a Protestant?

Rima By your bicycle. If it has a basket, you're the other side. They're always making chutney and giving it to Catholics. If they didn't poison us with their free soup during the Famine, they're going to do it now with their pots of preserve. I'm still worried about this boy. Why do you never speak?

Ned Me – sure I speak when I want to speak.

Rima Not you – I've been listening to you for years. I meant him.

Ned I know – I was making a joke.

Jamie Mam, you talk a lot.

Rima I do.

Jamie I don't say much. Between the two of us, we say what needs to be said. We're different. I like that. I don't wear makeup. I don't like guys. Marco does. Let him. I like difference.

Alec And you'll die fighting to prove it?

34

Jamie Yes.

Esther rises from the table and walks away.

Marco I love that boy. I'd marry him, but we're cousins. We'd need papal dispensation. I'd still love to ask his Holiness for that. It would be interesting to learn if the Pope's vocabulary includes the expression, 'Who the fuck is she?'

Esther
The King sits in Dunfirmline Town,
Drinking the blood red wine.

She is looking pensively into her wine glass.

Marco Is there more wine?

Justin pours Marco wine.

Rima Esther, don't sing. Dolly, don't let her. She knows sixty verses of the Green Glens of Antrim.

Alec Marco, you're on whiskey. Don't mix the grape and the grain.

Esther Don't worry. I dislike singing. I prefer the deaf and the dumb.

Anna Lizzie the dumbie's back on holidays from the special school in Dublin. They do great things with them. She's learned Irish dancing.

Rima That will keep her in shoe leather.

Justin Are you going to do what he tells you?

Marco What?

Justin Not drink the wine I poured you? Are you going to follow his orders? You don't have to. You're a free man here. The British army have no power in this part of the country.

Alec I'm out of uniform tonight, Justin.

Justin To my eyes you are always in uniform.

Marco Stay out of this, Justin.

Ned Justin, son, hold back like a good man.

Esther And turn out like you, Ned?

Ned There was a time it was good enough for you, Esther.

Esther Do you mind the time the cow shit lime and the monkey chewed tobacco?

Ned Have your say, Justin. The kitchen is yours.

Justin The kitchen's mine. The house is mine. And what's more, the port of Buncrana is mine. The ports of Ireland are ours, and ours alone. Look out there. That's what they want. The ports of our free neutral country. It is for them they want us in this war. They think they might still get us into it, because they believe – even after all they've done to us, all they've made us suffer, they still believe we could fear the Germans more than we hate the English. Alec, do you know how deeply you are hated?

Silence.

How deservedly you are hated?

Silence.

A bottle of rum, some wine – a drink over a table – so you think that will settle the difference between us? Have you no answer? Aren't you going to dazzle us with your British diplomacy? Or has that shit been scared out of you? What have you to face now? It's not a shower of Paddies with sticks and stones. It's the full might of Hitler's army. And you are going to lose the war.

Germany will win the war. The might of Hitler's army will win the war.

Alec Then God help you, Justin, and you know why. God help all of us about this table. There are millions dying because of the might of Hitler's army. And their sacrifice might save your skin, but I call what they're suffering a damned sight worse than whatever you and your people have suffered. God save Ireland, isn't that one of your country's battle cries? Do you know who will save Ireland this time? English conscripts, Welsh miners, Scottish shipbuilders, Irish navvies – that's who'll save Ireland.

Justin Go to hell.

Alec When I go off to fight in this war, hell is where I'll be heading into. And Justin, you won't be with me.

Justin Don't call me a coward.

Marco He didn't.

Justin Because I'm not.

Marco He didn't call you a coward.

Justin I am not a coward, Marco.

Marco I know.

Justin exits to the shore and lights a cigarette.

Alec Will he be all right?

Dolly Follow him, Ned.

Ned No.

Jamie Marco.

Marco I need some air. Excuse me. (*He goes out to the shore.*)

Ned How are you boys going to get back to barracks? Derry's fourteen miles away. The last train's gone a while ago. It's a long hike.

Alec I've the car.

Ned Will they get into hot water?

Alec Not if I'm with them.

Ned I hope you don't think I'm speaking out of turn, Alec, but you boys do need to watch yourself in this town. Justin keeps the fight to words. Others here will use their fists and feet. Buncrana is not the safest of towns for you. Stay in Derry. Stay across the border.

On the shore Marco takes Justin's cigarette from his lips. He lights his own with it.

Marco I like your hatred. Don't lose your hatred.

Justin What would you know about it?

Marco Everything.

Justin What would you know about me?

Marco What you've told me.

Justin What have I told you?

Marco Everything.

Marco touches Justin's face. Justin kisses Marco's hands.

Justin You'll tell no one else?

Marco Come back to the house. After me. I'm there.

Esther Very kind of you, Ned. We can all be kind. I'm sure my mother and sister will welcome you in here whenever you're on leave. Dolly?

Marco enters.

Dolly They'll all be welcome.

Esther Mother?

Rima is asleep.

Mother?

Dolly Has she fallen asleep? Mother.

Rima wakes up.

Rima I must have nodded off. I'm getting old. Were there any fights?

Dolly Yes.

Rima I missed them. Any good?

Alec Yes.

Dolly Justin does love his country, Alec.

Alec So he must hate mine?

Dolly Sometimes he must, yes. In the years you lived here, did you not find that out?

Alec No, I didn't. I never will. Do you want to see Hitler win, Dolly?

Justin enters as the evening light turns to blue and gold.

Dolly Once a year when I was living in Florence, I took the train to Ravenna. I wanted to see the mosaics in the churches. They're from the sixth century.

Rima Something's older than myself.

Dolly Ma, you would have loved them. The colour, the life in them. When I looked up at the walls and ceilings, for the first time I knew what it was like to have breath taken out of your body at the beauty of what your eyes saw.

39

Rima What did you see, daughter?

Dolly A procession of men and women. They were white and blue and gold, walking towards their God, and it was the walking that was their glory, for that made them human, still in this life, this life that I believe in. I believe in Ravenna. I remember it. I came home to Ireland, so I could remember it – there would be one in this country who would not forget in case Ravenna is destroyed. I think it's my life's purpose to say I saw it.

Rima God spare it.

Dolly I think I know what yours is, Alec. It's to fight, to save us from Hitler. It's a great purpose. I hope you win. I'm frightened you'll die. I'm frightened you'll lose.

Alec God save Ireland.

The sea sounds.

Act Two

SCENE ONE

It is three months later.
  *Rima is weeding in the garden, where she has placed
a chair.*
  Anna is washing potatoes.
  Ned sits morosely in the kitchen.
  *On the table there is a blue jug of milk, a slab of
butter and home-made bread.*

Anna You don't play tennis yourself, Mr Horgan?

Ned Do I look as if I play tennis?

Anna Mrs Horgan loves it. Her and Mr Justin have a
match every good morning. When the boys come down
at weekends on leave, they play what's called doubles. It
must be great fun. They're always breaking their hearts
laughing when they come home. Mrs West says it's doing
Esther the power of good. The exercise has taken years
off her.

Ned Did you call my wife Esther?

Anna I meant no disrespect.

Ned She's Mrs Horgan to you and your like. Just
remember where you crawled into this house from. You
can be sent post haste back there – if they'll have you.
Don't let yourself or this house down.

Anna I won't let them down and they won't send me
back to the convent.

Ned Then stop making sheep's eyes at that O'Brien fella.
I hope I haven't to remind you why you were reared in a

convent in the first place. It was the only place who would take you in. Your mother didn't want you. Your father didn't want her. Don't end up like that, Anna. You'll be barred from every decent house in this town.

Alec is by the shore.

Anna Maybe you should look to your own house.

Ned Do you want to feel the back of my hand?

Anna Could it be any harder than the back of the bitches' hands that reared me? Dear kind nuns? More like mad women. I am not afraid of the back of any man's hand. And maybe it's not me should be feeling yours.

Ned What are you saying?

Alec Good afternoon.

Ned Say nothing in front of the English stranger.

Alec enters the kitchen.

Alec I've just walked the five miles from Fahan. God, the White Strand. I do believe it's one of the great sights on this earth.

Ned You've seen a fair few of them, Alec.

Alec But it is truly magnificent on a clear day. When I was walking past the golf course at Lisfannon, I got it into my head, Neddy, we might play a few holes there.

Ned God, it's been years since I even set foot on the lower links.

Alec We hired a boat one year, Anna. We rowed from Fahan across to Fanad. Ned, Dolly, Esther, myself – the four of us. The sea – I'll never forget the blue.

Anna It must have been lovely.

Alec Like your eyes – that blue.

Ned We didn't hire the boat.

Alec Didn't we?

Ned It was my boat. Esther bought it for me as a birthday present. The first year we were married.

Alec How could I forget that? You were so proud of it. We joked about that. Ned's baby, that's what we christened it.

Ned We didn't. You christen a child, not a boat. You call a boat something. That's the correct word. You should know that, being English.

Alec I stand corrected. Apologies offered, old chap.

Alec salutes.

Ned Stop calling me that. I'm not old.

Alec I didn't mean –

Ned I'll take a walk round the shore front to see if these people are still at the tennis court.

Alec Will I stroll around with you?

Ned I can find my own way there. You don't have to lead me. Good day to you.

Ned leaves.

Alec What did I say to cause offence?

Anna How would I know?

Alec Were you two quarrelling when I came in?

Anna Why do you ask that?

Alec Well, your faces –

Anna I'm sorry our faces annoy you.

Alec Yours doesn't. It's a very pretty face.

Anna Pretty my arse.

Alec Anna, did I stumble on –

Anna Nothing – stumbled on nothing. What are you suggesting?

Alec I can say nothing right today. I don't seem to be saying what I mean. I did mean it about your eyes. There is the sea in them. Blue.

> *He touches her face.*
> *He kisses her.*
> *She laughs in his face.*

Anna You're an old man – old enough to be my father. (*She points at the dirty potato water.*) That's what you look like to me. Dirty. Not very pretty, am I? Not now.

Alec What's turned you sour like this?

Anna I was turned like this a long time ago. I know how to act sweet, but where's that getting me? I warn you – keep your hands to yourself. I'm no soft touch. I never was.

Rima Anna, would you fetch me a wee glass of milk?

Anna All right. Would you like a glass of milk as well?

> *He nods yes.*
> *Anna pours a glass of milk and hurls it over Alec.*

There's your milk.

> *She pours another glass of milk and takes it out to Rima.*
> *Alec towels his face with a dry dishcloth.*

Rima When is Dolly due back?

Anna She's late.

Rima She never had any notion of time. She wouldn't be caught by tides?

Anna She knows when they come in.

Rima This milk is nice.

Anna Lovely and cold.

Rima Like the Yank.

Anna I wouldn't know.

Rima You're growing into a fine woman. What you should do is get Dolly to teach you Italian. Go back there after the war's over.

Anna The war will never be over.

Rima Not for you – in this country. Too many long memories in Ireland. Leave it.

Anna You heard Ned's conversation –

Rima I hear everything. When I want to.

Anna Stop the weeding for today. You look tired. Will I sit and keep you company?

Rima You lazy wee bitch, get on and do your work. I know your like. We always had maids in this house. (*She gently pulls Anna to her and kisses her forehead.*) Good girl.

Anna What should I have said to Ned?

Rima What you did say.

Anna exits.
   Alec comes out to Rima.

There's an awful smell of spilt milk. Have you been crying, Alec? Running after young ones – did you think she would takes years off you? Leave her to the Yanks. Make an honest woman of Dolly.

45

Alec She wouldn't take me.

Rima You haven't asked her

Alec I know her answer.

Rima Isn't she wise then? Imagine being stuck with you making a pass after skirt that won't rise for you?

Alec Is that what happened to you and your husband?

Rima Who told you that – Dolly?

Alec I'm sorry – no – I shouldn't have –

Rima It was Ned then.

He nods his head.

That poor man's been dreading Esther will leave him since the day – hour they married.

Alec Will she?

Rima If she does she'll come back. Her father did. And he gave me a final gift – his son. That's why Justin is ten years younger than Dolly. He was always good at the giving – my man. Not just to me, but to all his fancy women. Still, there was enough to spare. I was left the house and a fair share of money. We were well off. Dolly could get to Trinity College –

Alec Where Catholics aren't supposed to go.

Rima Which is why she went. The same one was never Gospel greedy.

Alec Did he live to see his son Justin born?

Rima Just about. Sad that.

Alec Did Justin mind not having his father?

Rima Ask if I missed his father?

Alec Did you?

Rima I did, Alec.

Alec And you never –

Rima Strayed? No. When you give your heart and it's broken, you don't give it again. Well, I didn't anyway.

Alec Maybe I should make a pass at you, Rima?

Rima If I found a man's hand up my skirt now, I wouldn't know what he was looking for. Why don't you marry?

Alec My father – my mother –

Rima So?

Alec I didn't want to inflict the same unhappiness. Her crying like a lost child sitting on the bed beside me. Him walking the floor of their bedroom trying to make sense of what they'd done to each other. When she died, he kept on walking the floor – they should have separated long before they started living for the sole reason of hating each other. They kept on together – I'll never know why.

Rima We never know. I'll tell you a true story happened in this town. Two old women sitting drinking in a pub. In walked a beautiful young girl carrying a bunch of roses and wearing what looked like a brown dish cloth on her head. One old one – we'll call her Mary – she says, I swear to Christ that's the little flower, St Therese of Lisieux. The other one says, what would St Therese of Lisieux be doing in a pub in Buncrana? I swear it's her, Mary says. There's only way to find out, ask her. So Mary goes over and says to the young one with the dish cloth, excuse me, myself and my friend was wondering if you are the little flower, St Therese of Lisieux? The young one looks up from under the dish cloth and says, would you ever fuck off? Mary goes back and the friend says, is it her? Is it St Therese of Lisieux? Mary says, I asked her if she was the little flower and she told me to fuck off. That's a pity, says the friend, now we'll never know.

Alec And that happened in this town?

Rima Well, it didn't happen in Moville.

Alec Poor Moville.

Rima Moville my bollocks.

Alec You don't have bollocks, Rima.

Rima You haven't put your hand up my skirt – caught you there.

Alec You're an honest woman, Rima.

Rima I'm a bad bitch that says what she likes. Give me an honest answer to this, Alec. How's the war going to shape?

Alec It's touch and go.

Rima Still? The Germans?

Alec Mad.

Rima The English?

Alec Angry.

Rima The Yanks?

Alec Savage.

Rima Are they savage enough?

Alec Yes, they are.

Silence.

Rima And the Jews?

Silence.

Is it as bad –

Alec It's worse, I think. We don't know –

Rima We do.

Silence.

If any country should have opened the door to any people facing what they are facing – Ireland –

Alec It might not be as bad –

Rima We did nothing to save them.

Alec Ireland's a neutral country.

Rima Do you believe that?

Alec No.

Rima Neither do I.

Alec Rima, you welcomed Marco and Jamie. You welcomed me, an Englishman –

Rima Into Dolly West's kitchen. It's her that feeds you. Don't thank me.

Alec You reared her.

Rima That's right. Blame me. The old horse.

Alec I'm praising you.

Rima I prefer money. Now give my head peace, Alec. I hear the delightful roaring of the young people. Ask Dolly to marry you.

Alec I know her answer.

Rima Then turn back to Anna. Enjoy your milk bath, Cleopatra.

Alec You are a bad bitch, Rima.

Rima May you die roaring for a priest, you English heathen. Ask Dolly to marry you.

Alec exits to the shore.
    There is a short silence.
    It is broken by the sound of birds.
    Rima stands and looks about her. She is suddenly very tired. She sits down again.
    Justin, Esther, Marco and Jamie enter. They are in tennis whites.

Justin Christ, Ma, that was a great tennis match. You look tired. Are you all right? (*He kisses Rima.*)

Rima What was the score?

Justin First set, six–four to us. Second set, six–two to them. Third set, Esther, my, dear?

Esther Ten–eight, to us.

Justin I really thought I was going to go under. I got the racket in my hand and I played like a lunatic. No man was going to beat me. Ma, I wish you were there.

Rima And the score was?

Justin Ten–eight, yes. Ma, we were mighty. You should have seen us.

Esther I haven't a spark of breath left. They've killed me.

Justin Ten–eight, third set. Serving down the line, excellent advice, Esther.

Esther I'm going to die, Ma.

Justin We beat the Americans. We beat the Yanks, Esther. And they can really play, Ma. (*He lifts Rima into the air.*) Two hundred million of them – the best army on God's earth – and the Irish beat them.

Marco To punish myself I think I shall break a nail.

Justin Are yous starving? Do you want to eat before we swim?

Esther He wants to swim?

Marco He wants to eat?

Rima Dolly's left some bread and milk for you. Justin, son, swim and then eat.

Justin Come on, we'll hit the water, then we'll tackle the grub. (*He exits to the shore.*)

Marco Tennis, swimming, drill practice, dormitories – and to think my mother reared me to hate men. Tell me, do you think this kind of life is affecting me?

> *Marco grabs a tennis racket.*
> *He marches and performs expertly rifle drill with the racket.*
> *He suddenly drops the racket and shrieks.*

Don't look at me – don't look at me. (*He races off to the shore.*)

Rima When I met that young fella first, I thought he was mad. Now I think he's from somewhere on Mars.

Jamie Manhattan actually.

Rima God help Manhattan. Are they all like him? How did they let him live in New York?

Jamie By the expert use of his fist and feet. And he was well taught.

Esther Who by?

Jamie Me – the day I beat the shit out of him. Tough love. Learn to fight or die.

Rima Savage.

Jamie I had to be.

Rima Good.

Esther Aren't you the hard man?

Jamie When I have to be.

Esther And when you don't?

Jamie I'm not telling.

Rima Thank God for the good summer. It's not always that warm here. And the winters in Donegal are rough.

Jamie Not as rough as winter in New York. I like that time of year. You'd love the city then, Esther. We could skate together.

Esther I don't think I'd be too safe on the ice.

Jamie You would be with me. (*He takes her in his arms, dances with her, lifting her high into the air.*) See – you didn't fall. You were safe.

Esther I suppose so.

Jamie Come on, Esther, let's go for a swim. The water will be beautiful. Cold.

Esther Now I'm to do as you tell me?

Jamie If it makes you happy.

Esther Well, Ma, will I go for a swim?

Rima Stay here and keep me company. I've been on my own all day.

Esther The boss has spoken, Jamie.

Jamie All right. Good afternoon, ladies.

Rima God bless.

> *Jamie exits to the shore. Anna is waiting for him. Esther walks about the garden. Rima is looking silently into the garden.*

Anna Are you going for a walk along the shore?

Jamie I guess I am, Anna.

Anna You're always saying we should go for a walk.

Jamie I am?

Anna You know you are, God forgive you. What about today?

Jamie If you like.

Anna I like.

> *She gives him her arm and they walk together.*
> *Esther leaves down the newspaper.*

Esther Ma, what do you think has come over Justin? Do you remember even as a child he would nearly faint if anyone saw him in his drawers? Now every chance he gets, he's never out of those baggy shorts. What's happened to him?

> *Silence.*

I'm asking you what's happened to him?

Rima I'm sorry, I wasn't listening to you. I was looking at that patch in the garden where we grew pansies before the war. I always loved to look at them. They have magnificent colours.

> *Silence.*

Ned was looking for you.

Esther He knew where I was.

Rima He knew who you were with.

> *Silence.*

I said he knew who you were with.

Esther I'm sorry, I wasn't listening to you. I was looking at that patch in the garden where the piss-the-beds grew before the war. I never liked to look at them. They were useless to man or woman.

Silence.

I'm going in to read the papers.

Rima Maybe Justin's wearing shorts because somebody told him he had nice legs. Don't worry – it wasn't Jamie.

Esther Jamie?

Rima I meant to say Ned. So you're safe enough.

Esther I always will be.

She goes into the kitchen to read the paper.
Dolly enters pushing a wheelbarrow of mackerel and mussels.

Rima Jesus Christ, it's Molly Malone. (*She sings.*)
Crying cockles and mussels alive – alive o.

Dolly It was the only way to haul all this home. We have a houseful for the dinner tonight. I've mussels to start with, then there's mackerel.

Rima Is it only fish to eat? I think I'm turning into a mermaid. My arse will grow a tail soon.

Dolly It's good for you, mackerel.

Rima So's a beautiful big black man and I'm not seeing many of them.

Dolly I'll do my best to find you one.

Rima Do you know a man in Urris married a mermaid?

Dolly Urris men would marry anything.

Rima Don't you run down Urris. This man caught the mermaid in his nets. She granted him one wish. He wished she would grow legs, and they did grow long and beautiful on her. He took her ashore and he married her. They lived happily for a year and a day till their baby was born. Then she went back to the water with the human child and was never seen again. You see, he'd been tricked. She had caught him, not him her. So the Urris people believed. They have their own way. Very smart people, your father used to say. He loved Urris. Did all his fishing there. That man should never have been a doctor. He should never have come from money. Fishing – that's what he wanted to do. Your grandfather wouldn't hear of a son of his roughing it on a boat. But he loved the water. He knew Lough Swilly like the back of his hand.

Dolly I didn't know him, Ma. He left just after I was born. I didn't like him when he came back, and he died before I had time to change my mind.

Rima You're very hard on him.

Dolly Why did you marry my father, Ma?

Rima You better get these fish inside. They'll turn –

Dolly Why did you marry him? Why did you marry my father?

Rima You'd be better off asking why did he marry me. I was the blacksmith's daughter. Your grandfather wasn't too fond of that. He looked down his nose at the whole town. Your da, Paddy West, had bowed to him over the fishing. He didn't bow a second time. So we married and he tried his best to settle. But I was not the woman who should have been your father's wife. None of the others were either. Maybe your da should have married a mermaid, who would have left him after a year and a day.

Dolly But he came back to you, Ma.

Rima He came back to me, I saw his remorse. I said to myself, but not to him, too little, too late. That's changed. I forgive him now. And I forgive myself for what happened. What did happen? We had three children. Three good children. I love you all. You love me. Take care of each other.

Dolly What's brought this on?

Rima The lack of drink. Get in and fetch me a small whiskey. When I say small, I mean my small, not your small.

Dolly You want a large whiskey – just say what you mean.

Rima I say what I mean.

Dolly Do you want water in it?

Rima I do not, and I don't want herbs in it either.

Dolly You're getting herbs on your mackerel, like it or lump it.

Rima I'd love a bit of dulse from Urris. God, I can taste the salt. I'd love somebody would give me one wish. Do you know what I would be, Dolly? A big sea bird.

Dolly Are you sure you need this whiskey?

Rima I'd spread my white wings and I'd fly all over the world, China and India, starting here in Buncrana and then up to Malin Head, and I'd never touch the soil of Ireland again until I travelled the whole earth, landing back again in my own garden.

Dolly If you ever wondered why none of us were right in the head, just listen to yourself. (*She goes into the kitchen.*) Anything good in the paper?

Esther De Valera shit himself. What are you doing?

Dolly Pouring herself a whiskey.

Esther She's starting early.

Dolly Where is everybody?

Esther The boys are up swimming.

Dolly Is Alec with the lads?

Esther He might be.

Dolly Is Ned up with them?

Esther Why are you so worried about Ned?

Dolly I'm not.

Esther Neither am I.

Silence.

Mind your own business, Dolly.

Dolly Mind yours, Esther.

Esther Deliver the drink to the Queen of Sheba.

Dolly goes out to the garden.

Dolly Mammy, here's your whiskey.

Silence.

Ma, are you all right – are you sleeping?

Silence. She touches Rima.

Mamma.

The glass of whiskey falls from her hands. Silence.

Esther.

*Dolly enters the kitchen. She grabs Esther's hands.
A wail comes from Esther.
Darkness.*

Blue.

The closed coffin.

Esther, Dolly and Anna stand in mourning. Alec, in a black suit, stands by them.

Justin, Ned, Marco and Jamie are in uniform. The soldiers carry the coffin. The women and Alec follow it.

SCENE TWO

A seascape and shore.
It is evening, with signs of a storm mounting.
Justin and Marco are lying together.

Marco You can cry if you want to.

Justin I can't. If I start, I won't stop.

Marco takes his hand. Justin lets it go.

Not outside.

Silence.

Marco She knew you loved her.

Justin She knew I mocked her.

Marco She knew more. She knew about me and you.

Justin Did it kill her?

Marco No, it didn't.

Silence.

I don't have much time left in Derry. We're going to be fighting in Europe soon. Do you want me to go?

Justin I don't want you to die.

Marco Do you want me to go?

58

Justin In the evening that's in it, my mother's died, let me be, please, love.

Marco Love?

Justin Yes.

Marco Thank you.

Justin Thank you. What was I like before I met you? Twisted, miserable git. I'm so ashamed –

Marco Shut up you shmae.

Justin But what was I like?

Marco A Catholic bigot.

Justin Not all Catholics are bigots.

Marco They are where we're concerned.

Justin I once went to confession. I told this priest about myself. I was nearly shitting myself, Marco.

Marco Thank you for sharing that with me.

Justin The point is – he was a young priest, about my age. I think he believed I was trying to – you know. He started to tell me how much he loved women. How he'd love to get married. He went on and on. He wanted me to forgive him, because he couldn't help me. And I wanted to, but I couldn't, because I wanted –

Marco All I want from the Catholic church is an apology. A long apology. And I hope they will understand when I refuse to accept it.

Justin Too little, too late – my mother's old saying.

Marco She also used to say I was from Mars. I liked that. It showed she knew exactly what I was. And what was I like before I met you?

Justin Very smart, funny, a bit scary –

Marco A bit? I do not think so. Very scary. Twisted, mean cissy queen.

Justin Don't call yourself that.

Marco It's what my father called me every day until I kicked myself out of his house. I tried to live up to it.

Justin And your mother?

Marco Our Lady of Second Avenue? She once found some sketches I'd done of dresses when I was seven years old. She poured ketchup on every page, salt and lots of pepper. She made me eat them one by one until I vomited. I thought it was blood, the red coming up my throat.

Justin And you were a seven –

Marco – year-old cissy.

Justin You were a seven-year-old child.

Marco I hate her. I hate him. My mother. My father. Don't lose your hatred? Remember. I'm fighting this war because of hatred.

Justin And if you win, what happens then – what happens – do you stop hating? What difference –

Marco This difference. I will be able to look into the face of every man who fights beside me, and I will be able to say that in this war we fought on the same side against Hitler. Now you are fighting on Hitler's side because of your hatred of me and my kind.

Justin So your hatred of them will save you during this war?

Marco Don't lose your hatred. I told you. Hatred brought me to you.

Justin And only that?

Marco I'm the man from Mars, for God's sake. The loneliest man on the planet. I thought, till I met you. You were even lonelier. So I had to love you.

Justin kisses Marco.

Please, not here – not outside. Not when nobody's watching.

Justin I don't want you to go.

Marco When I come back, could we live in Italy?

Justin Jesus, yes. I'd love that. I've a bit of money from my father. Yes, Marco, yes. Dolly can teach me Italian. You're on. Where – what part of Italy?

Marco The Bronx?

Justin That's in New York.

Marco You poor boy, geography will be the death of you.

Justin Marco, you're to come home safe.

Marco Justin, I'm very frightened

Silence.

Justin You're to come home to me.

Marco I will, yes. (*He kisses Justin's hand.*) Twisted mean cissy queen.

Justin Fuck your mother, Marco.

Marco I did, before I left home.

Justin looks at Marco.

Does this mean you still want to marry me?

Justin It means you can't wear white.

Marco I could wear a kilt.

Justin You always do.

Marco And you love it.

They exit running.
Dolly enters, furious, followed by Ned.
The sky is darkening.

Dolly Keep that wife of yours away from me, or I'll swing this night for my sister if I see any more tears from her. That self-centred bitch is making so much mileage out of her grief, I'm beginning to wonder if she wanted my mother to die.

Ned Dolly, funerals are a funny business. They're worse than weddings. Families fight.

Dolly Put manners on that woman for once in your life, Ned, or I will – and it will be a sorry sight. In all the years I've come home, I've held my tongue about that bitch –

Ned My wife is a good woman.

Dolly You poor fool.

Ned Not where Esther's concerned.

Dolly Fool.

Ned I won't let you talk to me like that.

Dolly From me you'll hear the truth, Ned.

Ned You're saying what everybody's saying. Do you think I'm deaf –

Dolly Deaf and blind.

Ned I know the truth about me and Esther. Rima knew as well –

Dolly Rima took that young Yank into the house, and she knew what she was doing.

Ned Rima would never – to me – if I were to pray to her – in heaven –

Silence.

She loved me.

Dolly And to prove it she set you up to see if you were man enough –

Ned Man enough – dare any woman in this house doubt if I'm man enough? Do you know about your brother –

Dolly And the American soldier I hope he's fucking because he'll be doing more than his sisters have been doing? We know. Rima knew. She set that up as well. That's what she wanted. Stop saying prayers to that woman. She'd spit in your face rather than receive them. She believed in this world, not the next. She believed, God help us, in the three she's reared, and what have her two brave daughters done to honour her? One's barren because she couldn't tell the man she wanted that she did want him. And the other is barren –

Esther and Alec enter.

Ned Stop this chat.

Dolly Barren.

Esther Roar it louder, Dolly West. Let the whole town hear you.

Dolly The whole town knows it, Esther. What do you think they were whispering at the wake? When you were shaking their hands and crying in their arms, what were they saying behind our backs?

Esther I happen to think better of people –

Dolly You always have been a liar.

63

Esther The truth's coming out now.

Dolly You have always run rings around people and got away with everything, the way you did to my father.

Esther Back to that old jealousy.

Dolly You couldn't run rings around me or my mother.

Esther I've never tried that with anybody.

Dolly Then what are you doing to him – to Ned?

Alec Dolly, you'll regret –

Esther Regret what?

Dolly What do you think that young fella sees in you?

Esther What young fella?

Dolly Do I have to spell it out?

Esther Spell away. I've nothing to hide.

Ned She has nothing to hide – swear to God.

Dolly He sees a soft touch, a woman ripe for picking, an old woman.

Esther Stop it – make her stop it, Ned.

Ned Dolly, I'm warning you.

Dolly Daddy's girl has grown up into an old woman

Silence.

A sorry old woman. A foolish old woman. And in that she is like her sister.

Silence.

Esther I'll tell you what he sees in me.

Ned Stop, Esther, you're breaking my heart.

Esther He sees someone who cares if he lives or dies –

Ned I care about you.

Esther He sees someone he can make happy.

Ned Stop.

Esther He sees a woman whose heart and head have not grown too hard to say to him the kind of things you have said to me this night.

Ned Your good heart, Esther, would never let you say things like that to her.

Esther And I could, Ned. I know all about that – whore. And he as well – Alec knows – her whore master. But I never have, Dolly. And I have always told you the truth, Ned. I'm no liar.

Ned Esther, if you leave me, I may as well walk into the water.

Esther He's asked me. I've said no. Every night Jamie's down here he asks to meet me by the water. I say I might. God forgive me, Ned, I do say I might. But I never have. I never will. I won't leave you, Ned. Take me home. Take me out of that witch's sight.

Ned Dolly, fuck off out of our lives.

Esther The first time you said fuck, Ned. You know what to do.

Ned leads Esther off.

Alec What do you think you were doing?

Dolly Finishing what Rima West set in motion.

Alec Your mother –

Dolly Is at peace now. How do you like the Irish at war, Alec? We have a genius for it, but only when it's confined to our own. To save my family from destroying itself, you do not know what I would do. And if you want to stretch a point, you love your country and I do mine, as I love you, but if you and your Allies invade Ireland, I will be the first to put a bullet through your brain.

Alec Really? Well, we'd better not then. I won't anyway. I'm quite fond of my brain. Dear old noggin.

Dolly Are you trying to be funny?

Alec No – not funny. More amusing really. What the French call *amusant*. I'm sure the Italians have a word for it. Do tell me. By the way, you said you loved me.

Dolly I did not. I said I loved my country.

Alec And me. You love me. I distinctly heard you.

Dolly Alec, give my head peace. I've just buried my mother and lost my sister for life.

Alec Dolly, why did you never come home from Italy until you had to?

Silence.

Dolly Who do you think the men and women in the Ravenna mosaics were walking towards?

Alec Who?

Dolly Why do you think I opened a restaurant in Florence?

Alec Why?

Dolly She was the best cook.

Alec She never knew it.

Dolly I never said it. I had to leave her to prove it. Not until she died was I free to tell her.

Alec You loved her that much. Did you miss Rima there?

Dolly I missed you.

Silence broken by Dolly's sobbing, which she quickly stops.

What will I do if you die in this war?

Alec You'll find out soon.

Dolly It's happening – you're heading off to fight?

He nods.

So it's happening – the invasion?

Silence.

Ask me something.

Silence.

Ask me.

Silence.

The day I set eyes on you, I wanted you. Since you left me, I've been with you. Can you say the same?

Alec I can't, Dolly. And I can't believe you either. You've only wanted what you couldn't have. Is Esther really Daddy's girl? Or is that you?

Dolly He didn't want me. He didn't rear me. She did. Ask her.

Alec Yes. If I ever asked you to marry me, you would run a mile.

Dolly I'm standing still, Alec.

He takes Dolly hand. He moves it through his legs, up to both his breasts.
He kisses her hand.

What do you want? Woman or man?

Alec Both.

Dolly You can have that. (*She kisses him violently.*)

Alec What will I do if you die in this war?

Dolly You'll find out soon.

Alec Tonight.

Dolly This night.

> *Light fades on Alec and Dolly.*
> *There is thunder.*
> *Jamie comes from the darkness. He drinks from a bottle of whiskey.*
> *Anna also appears from the darkness.*

Anna Honest to God, old ones – wouldn't they turn your stomach?

> *Jamie takes a slug from the bottle.*

I might have a mouthful of that, if you'll let me.

> *He hands her the bottle. She drinks and chokes.*

Is this gin?

Jamie Whiskey.

Anna I only drink gin.

Jamie You don't drink at all, Anna. Why tell lies? I don't like lies.

Anna She's a liar, Esther Horgan is. Why blame me? Why want her? She's a married woman.

Jamie I don't any more.

Anna Wise man, stay away from married women.

Jamie And you should stay away from married men.

Anna You dirty beast – you're not.

Jamie Smart girl – I'm not.

Anna Why say you were and scare the daylights out of me?

Jamie Would it stop you if I were married, Anna?

Anna No, Jamie, it wouldn't. I would do anything for you. I'm dying about you.

Jamie Thanks, pal. Thanks. I've seen a man die. He was fighting for breath. Fighting for his life. He was my father.

Anna I never knew who my father was.

Jamie I didn't either. He didn't let me. But he held my hand when he was dying. I can't forget him breathing. Trying to say my name. I was called after him. He smelt like death. A smell of shit. And honey, the shit's scared out of me. I know I'm going to die. I'm going to die.

He begins to cry softly.

Anna I want to help you. Let me. (*She slips off her dress.*) Show me how to help you. You're going to live, Jamie. You're going to live.

They lie down together.
The storm erupts.
The sky starts to clear of the clouds' disturbance.

Act Three

SCENE ONE

Light only on in the kitchen.
It is dead of night.
In his shirt sleeves, Justin sits smoking a cigarette.
Esther enters in a dressing gown.

Esther I'll have to leave this house. I can't stay under the same roof as that woman. I'll have to go.

Justin You won't, Esther. Ned won't let you.

Silence.

Esther Is there any drink?

Justin Whiskey in my pocket.

She takes the bottle of whiskey from his coat pocket.
She pours herself a large drink.

A gift from Alex. They have their uses, the Brits.

Dolly enters.

Dolly I was out of order.

Silence.

I said things I regret.

Silence.

Esther The house is lonely without her. Do you know
I was always lonely here. Maybe if I left this house,
I would be less – Justin, our mother's dead. Our mother's
dead, Dolly. My mother is dead.

Dolly Yes, Esther.

Esther Lying in the cold clay of Cockhill graveyard. Lying there, not in her bed. Can you remember a night in this house she was not here? Do you remember us not sleeping, Dolly, listening to her at night, walking through the house, after our father left, waiting for him to come home.

Dolly Yes.

Esther He came home, and you were born, Justin.

Silence.

Teach me to cook.

Dolly Why?

Esther I wish to cook in my own kitchen. You'll leave with Alec, won't you? After the war I don't want to go hungry. Will you stay with him?

Dolly Will you stay with Ned?

Silence.

You will have a child.

Silence.

Justin Tell me the story, girls, about how I was born.

Esther Mammy was out in the garden.

Dolly She was planting flowers.

Esther And her waters broke.

Dolly She roared at the top of her voice –

Esther I have a son.

Dolly I know it's a son.

Justin And it was.

Esther Daddy had come home.

Dolly Mammy was happy.

SCENE TWO

It is after the war.
  Church bells.
  Suitcases and kit bags are packed, ready to go.
  In the garden, Ned is pushing a pram.

Ned
  And the sultan of Byzantium is laughing as they run,
  There is laughter in those fountains in the face of all
      men feared . . .
  It curbs the blood red crescent – blood red crescent –

  Silence.

How does the rest of that poem go, daughter dear? The
Battle of Lepanto. We won that, and the West was saved.
Somewhere near Venice, that's where Lepanto is. Some
day we'll go to Venice, pet, and walk on the water. We'll
see the moon in the sky, with one star beside it.

  He continues to push the pram.
    Alec is sitting alone on the shore.
    Dolly enters the shore.

Dolly I'm just going to take a last look at the grave.

  Silence.

It's looking grand. I'm sure Esther will tend it well.
Would you like to walk out with me?

Alec I've seen too many graves.

Dolly I know. Will you be all right?

  Silence.

What will you do till dinner time?

Silence.

Alec, you can't sit there like a lump looking into the ocean. Rouse yourself and have a walk. Do something. Even have a sleep.

Ned We've won. We've beaten them. Destroyed Hitler. May you never know his like.

Dolly Listen, I'm walking out to the graveyard. Do what you like, but if you're still perched here by the time I come back, I will put my boot up your hole and you'll move then.

She exits by the shore. Alec continues sitting. Ned is still pushing the pram. Esther enters the kitchen. She looks out and watches Alec.

Ned
There is laughter in those fountains in the face of all
    men feared – the face of all men feared –

*Unnoticed by Ned, Esther enters the garden.
Alec rises suddenly and shouts.*

Alec Dolly – wait for me, Dolly. (*He exits quickly.*)

Ned Dear girl, never know what we have known these past six years. Never have to fight the Battle of Lepanto.

Esther Never have to learn it – it's a rotten poem. What else are you whispering to the child?

Ned Babytalk – nonsense.

Esther You better practise it, Ned. The men home from the war – that's all you can say to them.

Ned They're like children, Esther. They've had a bad dream. We have to comfort them.

Esther Wee Patricia is all right?

Ned Grand.

He pushes the pram towards her. She pushes it back.

Esther Take the baby for a walk by the shore, Ned.

Ned Good sea air, good for her lungs.

Esther Perfect for her lungs.

Ned Perfect – isn't she?

Esther She is.

Ned I love her the way l love you.

Esther Stop.

Ned Irishmen are no good at compliments.

Esther They're not.

Ned Compliment – yes. Esther, do you remember how I asked you to marry me? I was too nervous to say it out straight, so I wrote to you. Would you do me the greatest compliment any woman could do to a man? You said yes. But I spelt it c-o-m-p-l-e-m-e-n-t. You told me to spell it right. I always learn from you.

Esther You do, Ned.

Ned I'll take the baby for a walk.

He goes off to the shore and exits.
Justin enters in his underwear, his trousers over his arm.

Justin Jesus, that man loves you.

Esther He does, yes. He does indeed. Would you put your trousers on in front of a lady?

He does so.

How's Marco?

Justin All right.

Esther The head?

Justin Not great.

Esther Jesus, this war has changed us all. What are we now, Justin?

Justin Managing.

Esther I had married the best of men. I didn't love him, I still don't. But he is still the best of men.

Justin The house is all yours.

Esther It was left to the three of us. I'll keep it safe. For you and Dolly – to visit when you like.

Justin Have you seen Jamie?

She shakes her head.

Esther He hasn't come down.

Justin Maybe he won't.

Esther That would be all right.

Marco enters, in pyjamas, agitated.

Marco Where were you?

Justin I haven't left the house.

Marco You said you would stay with me while I was sleeping. I woke up and you're not there.

Justin You seemed to be at peace.

Marco How would you know that?

Justin Marco, this is driving me stone mad. You're expecting me to watch over you twenty-four hours a day.

Marco I want to see you beside me. I don't want you to die.

Justin I'm not going to. The war's over. For Christ's sake it's over. The war is over.

Esther Marco, you're in Ireland. You're safe. You've had a bad dream –

Marco What I saw was no dream, lady. I know what I've seen. Justin, tell her.

Justin Esther, leave us. Just leave us.

Esther exits.

Marco What did that bitch mean? Dreams? The fucker –

Justin She's my sister.

Marco She didn't have to face what I had to face. I hate –

Justin Hate, you are full of it. You hate women, you hate men who love women –

Marco I fought better than any straight man.

Justin You fought the same as any straight man.

Silence.

Marco I saw the dead stretched like sheets of paper on the shore. White as paper. All dead. I have to vomit. Red sauce. All over the dead.

Justin It's blood, Marco.

Marco It's not.

Justin This time it was blood, red – red blood.

Marco All my dreams are red.

Justin Then you're going to have to stop dreaming. Because I will not live like this. I will not be your nursemaid in Italy. I know how hard it's going to be to manage there, and if we're going to survive together, then you will pull your own weight.

Marco The way you did during the war, Justin, holding the fort back in dear old Ireland. What a waste of time that was, for there was no one coming near you. You always knew you were safe so you let us suffer for you. If I'm full of hate, you and the Irish, you're full of shit. Shit.

Justin smashes his hand across Marco's mouth.

Justin The next time you open your dirty mouth, you apologise to me. You apologise. I have spent over a year not knowing anything about you. I have been waiting and willing you to come back to me. And to bring you home I would have done anything a man dared have done – I swear that. You talk about your dreams, Marco. What about mine? My dreams were full of you. Am I not the right fool? Because at heart you lack the guts to make this work by wanting to run back to New York, to Mammy and Daddy, and show them the cissy son is the suffering, conquering hero who's done his bit for Uncle Sam, and all will be forgiven. Run on back. Play at being Queen of the May. I won't be playing beside you. Good luck. May all your dreams be red.

Silence.

Marco That fucking colour never suited me.

Silence.

Justin You can wear anything.

Marco takes Justin's hand and rubs it gently across his lips.

Marco So we're going to Italy?

Justin Hold me back.

Marco Am I that full of hate?

Justin When you want to be.

Marco When I need to be. But not all the time?

Justin Not all the time.

Marco Justin, don't hit me again.

Justin I won't.

Marco Unless I tell you.

Jamie enters the kitchen.

Justin Is Anna not with you?

Jamie She's showing off her ring to some girls she knows.

Marco And the proud fiancé is not by her side?

Jamie I can't take the screams of joy.

Marco Come on, smile, Jamie – you're going to marry the girl.

Jamie And I'm sure my queer cousin wishes us well.

Marco I do.

Jamie And you Justin, our good fairy?

Justin Anna deserves all the luck in the world.

Jamie And she'll get that from me?

Justin She'll make you happy.

Jamie Yeah. Esther about?

Justin She was here a minute ago.

Jamie I'll wait for her.

Justin Ned and Esther are trying –

Ned enters the garden with the pram.

Jamie I need to talk to her.

Marco Justin, let him. It has to be done. Come on. I do want you to be happy, Jamie. Don't call Justin your good fairy. He's mine. And do not call me your queer cousin. The way the war's aged you. I look young enough to be your daughter. Ciao.

Marco and Justin exit.
Jamie lights a cigarette and enters the garden.

Jamie Look who's back, buddy boy.

Ned I can see for myself.

Jamie Why do I get the idea you're not pleased to see me?

Ned You tell me. Yanks know everything.

Jamie We knew how to win a war rather than sit on the sidelines shitting ourselves.

Ned My arse is clean.

Jamie Who wiped it for you?

Ned I'll wipe you, boy, once and for all.

Ned flattens Jamie.

Get up. I've not finished with you yet.

Jamie grabs Ned.
They fight fiercely, destroying the garden.
Esther rushes into the fight, fearing neither.

Esther What are you doing? Stop this – stop it now.

The fight stops at Esther's intervention.

What are the two of you playing at?

Jamie He's defending your virtue, Esther. We're fighting over you. (*He laughs.*) Christ, look at what we're fighting over. Is she worth it, Ned? She's already turned

79

into the bitter old bitch she deserves to be. On the streets of New York she couldn't give it away.

Ned I've given you a fair warning –

Esther I'll settle this. Not you. Get the child away.

Ned Tell him that it's my child. Tell him. It is my child, isn't it?

Jamie A bit of doubt, eh Ned boy?

Silence.

Ned Tell him. Tell me.

Esther That is my child.

Ned And mine – is it mine?

Esther You tell him, Jamie.

Silence.

Tell him the truth.

Jamie The child's yours.

Ned Will you get out of our lives now, O'Brien? Will you go back to your own country?

He exits to the garden, looks at the pram, and tries to walk away from it but can't.
He pushes the pram out.

Jamie Do you know what you've done?

Esther You've got Anna.

Jamie Leave her out of this. You're looking as though you hate me. Do you? Do you hate men?

Esther I don't think much of most of them.

Jamie You marry a man you despise. You pretend to want me, I fall for it and you –

80

Esther Walk away. Back to where I started.

Jamie Why?

Esther I'm my father's daughter. We tend to leave people we love.

Jamie You love me?

Esther Yes. But I've lost you. And you've lost me. That's why you want me. That's what hurts you.

Jamie And that's what you enjoy.

Esther No, Jamie. You haven't been listening to me. If you had, you would have heard my heart breaking.

Jamie Esther –

Esther I know what I'm doing. I know what's for the best.

Anna enters from the garden.

And here's the best girl you could get. Anna pet, have you been up the town showing off your sparkler? Let me see it again. It is a beautiful ring.

Anna Everybody says it's the last word.

Esther Congratulations again, to you both.

Anna Thanks, Mrs Horgan.

Esther Less of the Mrs Horgan. You don't work for us any more. It's Esther you call me now. And you've to promise to write from America.

Anna I will, Esther, and I promise to sign it Mrs Jamie O'Brien. (*She laughs.*) It still sounds wild funny. I'll never get used to it.

Esther You will. We all do. I've a dinner to put on the table. We'll eat soon. Thank God that sister of mine's taught me about cooking. If she hadn't, my husband might starve to death.

Anna Where is Miss West – Dolly? I want her to see the ring.

Esther Out walking the town with Alec.

Anna Is he ever going to get better? Will he ever talk to anybody again?

Esther He talks to Dolly. He'll talk to us all in time. (*She exits.*)

Anna Jamie, thank Christ the war didn't drive you mad.

Jamie I had you to come home to.

Anna Me? You had her to come home to. So, she's turned you down. Think I don't know? Well, I'm not proud. I'll take her leavings. You're worth having. (*She kisses him.*) You like them tough, don't you? You think she's tough. I'm tougher. I've had to be. Now, will I enjoy New York?

Jamie You were made for each other.

Anna Just like us.

Jamie You think so?

Anna I know so.

Jamie And if we turn into Esther and Ned?

Anna We'll say a little prayer that we won't. I really want to say a prayer. A quick trip to the chapel. It will be the last time I'll see it. I will never, ever come back here. And neither will you. I'll see to that.

> *Jamie and Anna exit.*
> *The kitchen goes into half-light.*
> *Alec and Dolly enter the shore.*

Dolly Alec, I can't live in England. Why are you asking me to do that? There's better ways of leaving me, man.

Alec I have to live there.

Dolly You've never settled there before. Why would you now?

Alec The war. What I saw.

Dolly Are you going to tell me what you went through?

Alec No.

Dolly You will have to, if you're to get me to live in England.

Alec I can't.

Silence.

Dolly Alec, tell me what you saw.

Alec Children. Dead children. Burned off the face of the earth. Millions. They saved us. The innocent. I walk through this town –

Dolly Buncrana.

Alec That's never known a war. That's never lost its young. I hope it never does.

Dolly If we ever do, it will be our own doing.

Alec Would you do that to each other?

Dolly Alec, after what you've seen do you not know what we're all capable of doing?

Alec She knew – Rima knew what was being done. Don't ask me how – Maybe it killed her.

Dolly No, Alec, she just died – she died happy.

Alec She died knowing –

Dolly Alec, why do you want to live in England?

Alec It's my home. I need to go home. What's been inflicted on it. It's hungry. Bombed, broken, lost. England, on its knees. Poor country.

Dolly Begging for bread.

Alec Hungry.

Dolly Poor country.

Alec Lost. I have to go there.

Dolly We're going there then.

Alec Will it kill you?

Dolly You will.

Alec You can say no.

Dolly Can I? I don't think so.

Alec You might love it.

Dolly No, Alec, I won't love it. They won't love me. I'll make sure of that. That is your country. Yes, it has suffered. Yes, it's on its knees. But I am not. All right, I'll stand by you. But I'll be standing on my own two feet. And I'll be doing it for you. Not your country.

Alec (*speaks*)
I vow to thee my country, all earthly things above,
Entire and whole and perfect the service of my love.
The love that asks no questions, the love that stands
   the test,
That lays upon the altar, the dearest and the best.

He sings.

The love that never falters, the love that pays the price.
The love that makes undaunted – the final sacrifice.

Through the hymn, light rises on the kitchen.
   Esther is carving a leg of lamb.
   Marco, fully dressed, is sitting beside Justin.
   Jamie sits, Anna behind him, her arms about him.
   Ned is in the garden, looking at the child in the
pram.
   Dolly speaks.

Dolly
   And there is another country, I've heard of long ago,
   Most dear to them that love her, most great to them
      that know.
   We may not count her armies, we may not see her king,
   Her fortress is a faithful heart, her pride is suffering,
   And soul by soul and silently, her shining bounds
      increase,
   And her ways are ways of gentleness and all her paths
      are peace.

Esther Ned, come in.

Alec Gentleness.

Esther Dolly, Alec, the lamb's ready.

Alec Peace.

Esther Pour the wine, Justin. Pass the bread, Anna.

   They do so.
   Ned stays in the garden, looking in.

Alec Is the war over, Dolly?

   Justin, Marco, Anna and Jamie click glasses.

Dolly I hope so.

Justin For richer or poorer – in sickness and in health –
till death us do part.

Alec Is the war over?

Dolly I said I hope so.